He shoots...

Saved!!

This will beat him!

Gromit and snowman!

Me and Piella.

Mmmm crackers.

CONTENTS

Published 2010. Pedigree Books Ltd
Beech Hill House, Walnut Gardens, Exeter, Devon EX4 4DH
books@pedigreegroup.co.uk | www.pedigreebooks.com

£12.99

Welcome to the World of Wallace and Gromit!

One of England's much-loved double acts,
Wallace and Gromit are a mainstay of British humour.

Whether it be quirky Wallace's insane inventions or the inevitable capers that ensue in the aftermath of his tinkering, the pair are loveable and amusing.

From flying to the moon to sample some exotic cheese to falling in love with almost every woman he meets, Wallace relies on his loyal sidekick Gromit to keep him in check and, more often than not, save him from disaster!

Gromit doesn't talk, but is highly intelligent, and displays infinite courage and bravery when it comes to rescuing his master.

They've come up against the likes of Feathers McGraw, Preston the evil dog and Piella Bakewell also known as 'the Cereal Killer', but the daring duo have always come out unscathed... just!

But, despite their dramatic escapades, at heart the characters are just a homely man and his best friend, his dog.

You can read more about the main characters in their profile pages later on in this annual.

Crazy Creations!

As anyone who has ever watched Wallace and Gromit can testify, Wallace is full of ideas – whether they be good or otherwise!

Always tinkering, the kind-hearted Wallace invents various contraptions to aid household chores and tasks.

Take the device that wakes Wallace up in the morning, sliding him out of his bed straight into the clothes he will wear that day and seating him at the dining room table, ready for breakfast!

Here are some of Wallace's other inventions, as well as the real-life ideas that might have provoked Wallace to make them.

The Turbo Diner

A luxury upgrade to a ready meal, this invention is an answer to the microwave. Rather than producing a television meal, though, it serves up a feast!

The microwave oven was discovered by accident, by an American engineer! Working on radars in 1945, he found that a chocolate bar he had packed for his lunch starting to melt.

Noticing this, he extended this to other foods. In 1947, the company he worked for created the first microwave oven, the Radarange – which was almost six foot high, the size of an average man!

Read the results of Wallace's ingenious cure to kitchen nightmares on page 82.

The 525 Crackervac

A vacuum cleaner with a difference!

Frustrated by the mess that his favourite meal – crackers and cheese – produces, Wallace decides to tackle this with a classic invention – the 525 Crackervac.

Built with an automatic cracker detector installed inside it, the vacuum will instantly clean away cracker crumbs.

The first vacuum cleaner was built as long ago as 1860, by an American man called Daniel Hess. Though he described it as a carpet sweeper, it was the first version of a vacuum.

See the unexpected results of the Crackervac on page 53.

The Bullyproof Vest

As its name suggests, Wallace was inspired by the bulletproof vest for this invention – a gadget designed to ward off bullies or burglars with the press of a button.

Tested extensively by Gromit, bless him, Wallace has his contraption down to a tee: no one will want to mess with him when he's wearing this device!

The design of bulletproof vests has gone on throughout the ages, whenever there has been conflict.

The first example of a piece of armour being worn to absorb the damage of gunfire was in 1561, when Maximilian II (a Roman Emperor and king of various countries) was devising a garment that could reduce damage caused by a weapon.

For more on Wallace's take on the bulletproof vest, turn to page 117.

Wallace,
the Nation's Greatest Inventor!

Widely hailed as one of the nation's greatest inventors, WALLACE is responsible for a wide range of contraptions designed to make life a bit easier or to get rich quick. But however well-intentioned his ideas are, they inevitably end up leading to trouble for him and his faithful dog Gromit. He is distinguished by a fondness for cheese and crackers, and rather questionable taste in knitwear.

Despite his dapper demeanour, Wallace has always been unlucky in love – his failed romances include wool-shop owner Wendolene, the gracious Lady Tottington and the scheming Piella Bakewell. Just as well he's got his loyal companion Gromit to console him when the course of true love fails to run smoothly.

Yes, through thick and thin, Gromit is always by Wallace's side, and together they have been on a series of memorable, if unintentional, adventures.

Wallace's gadgets help him through every stage of the day – from getting up in the morning to buttering his toast to going for a spin on his motorcycle. But, as Gromit would readily admit, they usually end up making things worse rather than better.

But when things go wrong, Wallace can always comfort himself with a nice slice of Wensleydale cheese and a cup of tea.

He is very particular about his appearance, and is the proud owner of a hair-dryer, even though these days he is completely bald.

"GET THE KETTLE ON LAD ITS NEARLY 4 O'CLOCK!"

Mix and Match!

Wallace's inventions take him and Gromit on all sorts of adventures, can you match the pictures to the correct description?

1 Moon Rocket

Exasperated by his lack of cheese, Wallace decides to take Gromit on holiday to a place where his favourite foodstuff is said to be in plentiful supply – the Moon! He builds a rocket in his basement and packs it with plenty of crackers before take-off.

A) 2

D) 6

4 Feathers McGraw

This seemingly innocent penguin turned up as Wallace's lodger when he decided to rent out a room. But disguised as a chicken with a rubber glove on his head, he in fact proved to be a sinister jewel thief on the run.

2 Techno Trousers

Wallace ordered these from NASA and adapted them into a dog-walking machine for Gromit's birthday. But the trouble they saved him was nothing compared to the chaos that was caused when they fell into the wrong hands.

B) 5

C) P

5 Preston

When Wallace fell in love with Wendolene Ramsbottom, he had no idea that her faithful dog Preston was in reality an evil robot, with a sinister agenda which ended up threatening to turn both the lovebirds, as well as Gromit and Shaun The Sheep into dog food.

3 Porridge Gun

Designed to serve up a healthy breakfast at the start of the day, this contraption proved itself a very handy combat weapon against one of Wallace and Gromit's more menacing enemies.

C) 4

F) 3

6 The Cooker

A stickler for tidiness, the Cooker was none too impressed when he discovered the remains of Wallace and Gromit's picnic, so he slapped a parking ticket on them. You can't blame him really – all he wanted to do was enjoy a bit of skiing.

Easy Cheesy!

Wallace is a cheese enthusiast. Though his favourite is Wensleydale, he's also partial to a bit of Gorgonzola or even moon cheese! See if you can find the ten different varieties of cheese in the wordsearch below.

well done lad

C	R	O	Q	U	E	F	O	R	T	O	T	O
H	E	W	E	N	S	L	E	Y	G	C	O	M
E	C	L	Z	Z	O	M	P	A	O	R	O	R
L	H	B	A	Z	Z	A	R	Z	R	P	A	O
A	E	R	P	D	M	O	Z	Z	G	A	A	R
D	D	I	A	O	E	A	R	O	O	R	R	R
Y	D	A	R	V	R	V	E	M	N	M	R	M
E	D	Z	M	E	R	B	O	L	Z	E	E	E
L	R	Z	L	D	F	L	I	D	O	Z	L	L
S	R	L	L	A	Z	O	M	A	L	Z	Z	L
N	A	S	E	M	R	A	P	L	A	E	A	E
E	C	H	E	E	S	M	O	Z	Z	L	L	L
W	E	S	E	E	H	C	N	O	O	M	M	M
T	R	A	D	D	E	R	S	T	I	L	L	L
S	T	A	Z	E	K	L	A	B	R	S	S	S
S	N	O	D	S	R	A	R	R	O	T	T	T
Z	T	G	R	D	M	E	P	I	Q	I	I	I
O	E	Y	G	E	E	A	Z	E	U	L	L	L
L	L	E	O	Z	Q	H	Z	O	E	M	M	M
A	L	O	P	A	R	M	C	M	F	O	O	O
M	O	S	T	I	L	T	O	N	O	P	P	P

Key:

- ☑ Wensleydale
- ☑ Moon Cheese
- ☑ Gorgonzola
- ☑ Stilton
- ☑ Cheddar
- ☑ Dovedale
- ☑ Brie
- ☑ Mozzarella
- ☑ Parmesan
- ☑ Roquefort

Gromit,
Man's Best Friend

Doggedly devoted to his owner, GROMIT keeps a wary eye on Wallace's more madcap schemes. Gromit prefers the quiet life – his favourite hobbies include reading, knitting and listening to classical music – but when one of Wallace's crazy inventions gets out of hand, he is forced to become the hero and save the day. While Wallace may be the Master, Gromit is definitely the one with the mind.

In an ideal world, Gromit would devote his time to looking after his master Wallace and enjoying a bit of peace and quiet so he can get on with reading a book or doing the crossword. But with Wallace forever cooking up crazy ideas, the chances of that happening are pretty slim.

Gromit is the perfect household companion, happy to serve his master by doing the cooking, cleaning and shopping without complaint, even if Wallace does tend to take him for granted.

But when one of Wallace's contraptions leads to disaster, Gromit shows that he is made of sterner stuff – he can pilot an aircraft, steer a hot-air balloon and foil a deadly jewel thief when the occasion calls for it.

While Gromit enjoys the solitary life, he is not beyond finding a little time for romance. During their most recent adventure, he found himself falling for the timid and vulnerable poodle, Fluffles, and rescuing her from her cruel mistress Piella Bakewell. In fact, his romance fared a lot better than Wallace's love for the murderous Piella did.

But at the end of the day, Gromit's true loyalty is to his master. Brave, devoted and multi-talented, he really does prove that a dog is Man's Best Friend.

"LOVE IS A MANY SPLENDORED THING GROMIT, BUT IT DOESN'T HALF TIRE YOU OUT - I AM CREAM CRACKERED!"

THE EVENING LAMP POST

spate of **B**iscu**i**t thefts, too.

One victim was the local **b**aker, who came into work one morning to find all of his **I**ced **b**uns missing.

Speaking to our reporter, the baker said: "I am distraught, what will the people have for **L**unch now?"

Our advice would be to **I**ock up your **C**onfect**i**onery and be on **G**uard at all times.

Exclu**S**ive news reaching us here at The E**V**enin**G** Post suggests that there is a cake **t**hie**f** in the area!

The sweet **S**oothe**d** crook is keen on **C**upcakes and **M**u**ff**ins, while he has also been linked to

PUZZLE PAGE

SUDOKU

Each Sudoku has a unique solution that can be reached logically without guessing. Enter digits from 1 to 9 into the blank spaces. Every row must contain one of each digit. So must every column, as must every 3x3 square.

4	7	3	6	1	2	8	5	9
5	2	9	3	7	8	4	6	1
6	1	8	5	4	9	2	7	3
3	9	7		2		6		
8	5	2	4	6	1	9	3	
4	4	6		9				
		5		3			1	
2			1					
	6			8	7	3		5

CROSSWORD

Down:
1. One of Gromit's favourite pastimes, though we never see him wearing his creations! (8)
3. The sheep that Gromit befriended in A Close Shave. (5)
4. Among his prized possessions, this helps him to wake up in the morning! (5/5)
5. Gromit's friend Hutch is what kind of animal? (6)

Across:
2. Having just woken up, Gromit would probably read this with his breakfast. (9)
6. Like most dogs, Gromit loves one of these! (4)

Gromit's favourite section in the newspaper is the Puzzle Page, and he prides himself on being an expert at crosswords and Sudoku. See if you can challenge Gromit to become the West Wallaby Puzzle Champ with the teasers above...

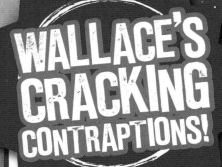
THE SNOWMAN-O-TRON

Christmas is coming and the snow is falling. But what happens when the festive spirit gives way to the competitive spirit…?

When the local paper announces its annual snowman-building competition, Gromit decides that this year he is going to be the winner.

He spends hours delicately carving a splendid snow sculpture – which, on closer inspection, seems to bear a striking resemblance to his master…

But his efforts are disturbed when Wallace arrives riding on his latest contraption, determined to win the snowman competition too.

The Snowman-O-Tron scoops up snow into its compacting compartment and in moments…

… Out pops a ready-made snowman – which unfortunately trashes Gromit's snow-sculpture in the process.

"Not bad for a first try," Wallace announces to his horrified pooch. "I think I've captured the inner snowman".

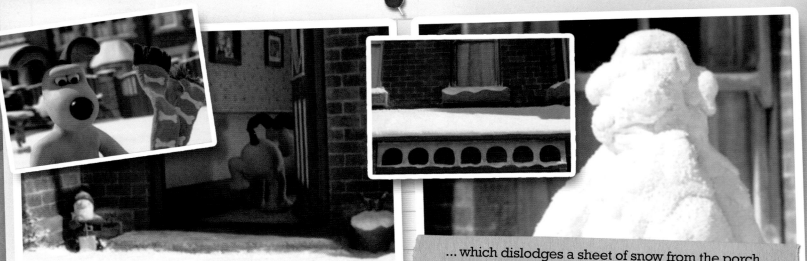

Flabbergasted to see all his hard work destroyed, Gromit storms back into the house, slamming the door behind him...

... which dislodges a sheet of snow from the porch, completely covering Wallace who is still admiring the Snowman-O-Tron's creation. Wallace is frozen to the spot – quite literally!

A few hasty additions and Gromit reaches for his camera...

... Snapping his snow-covered master as his entry into the competition.

Sure enough, the photo wins first prize. "Well done, lad," says a grudging Wallace...

"But if you ask me, that snowman was abominable!"

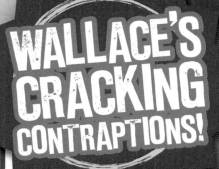

WALLACE'S CRACKING CONTRAPTIONS!

THE CHRISTMAS CARDOMATIC

Ever get the feeling that Christmas card manufacturers are 'Robin' you blind? Wallace does, so he's come up with a way to make them on the 'Cheep'!

"Watch the birdie!" cries an excited Wallace as a gigantic robin strikes a series of festive poses in front of a wintery backdrop.

"Say cheese!" he says, taking one final snapshot. "Okay," he chuckles, "that's a wrap!"

But as the photo shoot comes to an end, the robin slips over backwards on the artificial snow...

And its head falls off to reveal a rather disgruntled Gromit underneath the feathery costume.

The camera work done, Wallace turns his attention to his latest invention – The Christmas Card-O-Matic.

A little glue and a sprinkle of glitter and the machine chugs into action, producing cards with the images from Wallace's camera.

"Everything seems to be developing nicely," he observes as the first card trundles out of the machine.

"I think we've captured the true spirit of Christmas," says a delighted Wallace as he admires his handiwork.

But Gromit's not so sure – to him, it looks more like a dog in a robin costume falling over backwards!

"You'd never get a scene like that, not in a month of Sundays," boasts Wallace as he pulls up the backdrop...

...Revealing a wintery West Wallaby Street through the window behind. Gromit looks in amazement at the scene...

...A true Winter Wonderland with real robins frolicking in real snow. But Wallace is oblivious – "Come on Gromit," he calls, "it's your turn to lick the stamps!"

ROAD TRIP

62 WEST WALLABY STREET...

It's like I always say, *Gromit,* wherever I wander...

... there's no place like *home!*

It's a rare honour, being invited to give a talk at Lord Locan's *School For Precocious Upstarts.*

Good thing we have no trouble with the short notice, eh?

Ever ready, that's us!

Right then, Gromit – get that *show and tell* stuff stowed properly...

... and get the *kettle* on!

No time for a *sit-down* breakfast, we've a long drive ahead of us.

So... we'll have it *on the go!*

Oh, and one more little improvisation... the *home-xpress* comes with an *autopilot* facility, for tricky manoeuvring and parking. Here...

... I'll demonstrate!

Oo-er...

SCREEECHHHH

... it's not supposed to do *that!*

HONK
HONK
HONK

HOOOONK!

HONK

Shriek!

SREEE! VREEK

DRRING DRRING DRRING

DRRING DRRING

DRRING

Gromit? It's *Wallace.* listen carefully...

...Something's interfering with the *signal* from the remote control.

The radio frequencies must be cancelling each other out. Gromit...

... try *changing* the station...

MUFFIN

KLK!

ZZZ-WHRRRR

KLK!

CRUMPET TOAST MUFFIN HOT BUN

Well done, Gromit. I think you've—

Oo er...

FLUSSH

He's in the *mega-mart!* And, oh...

... *that's* a good offer. We're a bit low on *double gloucester!*

BUY ONE - GET ONE FREE ENGLISH CHEESES!

CAR WASH

SST-POP!

KLK WRRRR!

Eh! I've a got a clear signal! Gromit must have *fixed* the problem. Well, lad...

ROAD CLOSED

... I'm *back* in charge!

Gromit!

I can't stop you in time! do something...

... *anything!*

K'LK!

MUFFIN   HOT CRO... BUN

ZZ-RRTCH

WHOOF

Ah, um. Well...

... at least you've got some *drag!*

LATER...

Excellent talk, Wallace, *excellent.* Care to join us for a spot of lunch.

Oh, er... no, thank you...

...we'd better be getting back. Long drive and all that. We'll eat lunch *in transit.*

Ah, mm...

"... ANYONE SEEN *GROMIT?*"

JOURNEY'S END!

...VOLCANO!

TIMESCALE

IMPRESS YOUR FRIENDS WITH YOUR VERY OWN ERUPTING VOLCANO!

EASY / HARD

How to do it:

What you will need:

- Bottle of fizzy pop (or water)
- Baking soda
- Vinegar
- Cereal box
- Newspaper
- Glue
- Paint brush/paint
- Sellotape

1. This one is really effective! All you will need to do is get a small bottle of fizzy pop (or water) and stand it on the unfolded cereal box or other suitable cardboard.

2. Crumple up pieces of newspaper and make a base for the volcano around the bottle. Use tape to tape down the paper. Continue by cutting strips of newspaper and sticking them to the sides all around the bottle.

3. Water down the glue slightly first, then paint the strips with the gluey paste using your paintbrush.
Place your strips one at a time and smooth down to remove air bubbles. Cover with two to three layers at a time until you have a general shape of a mountain. Don't put too many on at once or it will take too long to dry.

4. Once it has dried, you can paint the sculpture to look like a volcano. Colour the main body of the volcano (the area around the bottle) brown, for instance, have orange lava spilling down one side... be creative!

5. When that has dried, put some baking soda in the bottle and then add vinegar. These two ingredients react together to form carbon dioxide which will 'erupt' from the bottle like a volcano!

VINEGAR

BAKING SODA

FIZZYPOP BOTTLE

NEWSPAPER CRUMPLED

NEWSPAPER STRIPS

CARD

TIMESCALE

...MUSICAL INSTRUMENT!

BECOME A MUSICAL GENIUS FROM THE COMFORT OF YOUR OWN HOME, BY CREATING YOUR OWN WATER-BASED MUSICAL INSTRUMENT!

EASY | | | | HARD

What you will need:

- Water
- Three or four glasses
- Metal spoon
- Measuring jug

How to do it:

1. Firstly, make sure you have an adult helping you with this one - especially when carrying and holding the glasses.

2. Using the measuring jug, you will need to fill each of your three or four (or more!) glasses with water, but to a different level.

3. Have one glass almost full, another almost empty and another somewhere in between!

4. Place the containers on a table and gently tap the rim of each glass with the metal spoon. This should produce sounds of different pitch from each glass.

5. If you can get the hang of it, you may even be able to play your own tunes on the glasses!

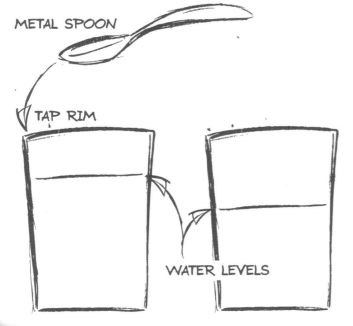

METAL SPOON

TAP RIM

WATER LEVELS

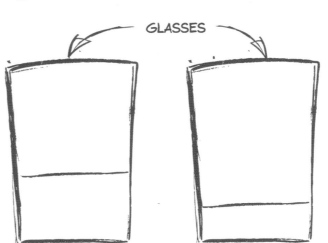

GLASSES

MAKE YOUR OWN... ...ROCKET!

SEE YOUR VERY OWN HANDMADE ROCKET SOAR OFF INTO THE SKY!

How to do it:

EASY   HARD

What you will need:

- Empty fizzy pop bottle
- Paper and pencils
- Cardboard
- Glue
- Scissors
- Sellotape
- Bike pump
- Bicycle inner tube
- Drill (with adult supervision)

1. Take an old fizzy pop bottle, using paper and/or card, decorate the bottle in a spaceship theme by wrapping the paper/card around the bottle and Sellotaping or gluing it down.

2. Cut two triangles of cardboard and glue them to either side of the bottle as wings. Make sure you use the bottom of the bottle as the top of your design! This will become clear in a moment...

3. Cut the valve away from the bicycle inner tube to use for your rocket launcher. With the help of an adult, drill a hole in a cork and push the valve through this.

4. Fill the bottle half way with water and wedge the cork firmly into the bottle. Now connect your bike pump to the inner tube and pump the bottle full of air until it flies off into the sky!

ROCKET

CORK

INNER TUBE VALVE

SAFE LAUNCH AREA

BIKE PUMP

CORK

Note: Be careful when doing this. Make sure you don't set your rocket off near any windows or greenhouses and make sure you take cover when the rocket comes back to land!

...QUICKSAND!

TIMESCALE

EVER FANCIED SEEING YOUR SINDY DOLL OR FOOTBALL FIGURE SINK? WE'VE GOT THE PERFECT QUICK SAND TRAP.

EASY — HARD

What you will need:

- Biscuit Tin
- Scissors
- Gravel
- Hose
- Sand
- Sindy Doll
  (or equivalent)

How to do it:

1. Ask an adult to cut two holes in a biscuit tin, one at the bottom and another on the side. These should be around 25mm in area.

2. Fill the hole in the base of the tin with the gravel, to stop the sand (which you'll add in a moment) falling through it.

3. Fill the tin with sand (up to the level of the hole in the side) and place doll on top.

4. Now put your hose into the side hole and turn it on. The water will flow down through the sand, which will make the sand compact.

5. Then switch the hose to the bottom hole, therefore creating an underground spring, and watch the doll sink into oblivion!

UNFORTUNATE DOLL

SAND FILLED BISCUIT TIN

GRAVEL

WATER HOSE

Wallace and Gromit's QUIZ! PART1

DO YOU REMEMBER WALLACE'S INVENTIONS? FROM FLYING TO THE MOON TO MAKING DOG WALKS EASIER, THE EAGER INVENTOR CERTAINLY HAS A VARIETY OF IDEAS. SEE HOW WELL YOU REMEMBER THEM?

Q1 Wallace gave Gromit 'The Wrong Trousers' for his birthday, what was the other gift he gave to his loyal pet?

Q2 A former NASA product, what were the trousers' original name?

Q3 When Wallace and Gromit flew to the moon in 'A Grand Day Out', where did they build the rocket?

Q4 Why was the moon their chosen destination?

Q6 What unfortunate sheep fell victim to that machine?

Question 5
Along with the Wash-O-Matic, what other invention had Wallace conjured in 'A Close Shave'?

Q7 Who alters the Wrong Trousers for devious means?

Q8 What were these devious means?

Q11 What is Wallace doing when the Wrong Trousers are being controlled by his new tenant, the Penguin?

Q9 What character do Wallace and Gromit encounter while on the moon?

Q12 Wallace falls in love with Wendolene Ramsbottom, what is the name of her evil dog?

Q13 What allergy means that Wallace and Wendolene can't be together?

Question 14
Gromit falls in love in 'A Matter of Loaf and Death', who is the object of his desire?

Question 10
What dream does this character develop after finding a left-over magazine?

HOW TO WIN FRIENDS AND INFLUENCE POODLES

YOUR SCORE
..... /14

Wallace and Gromit's QUIZ! PART 2

PART TWO OF OUR ULTIMATE WALLACE AND GROMIT QUIZ FOCUSES ON WALLACE'S CRACKING CONTRAPTIONS. HOW MUCH DO YOU REMEMBER ABOUT OUR FAVOURITE INVENTOR'S CREATIONS?

Question 1
What contraption does Wallace come up with to make ready-made Christmas cards?

Q2 And what outfit does Gromit have to wear for these cards?

Q3 What meal does Wallace ask the Autochef to serve Gromit?

Q4 What food is 'Shopper 13' sent to collect from the local shop?

Q5 What machine did Wallace come up with to help improve his football skills?

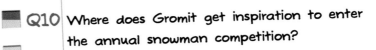

Q11 What is Gromit's final entry for that competition?

Question 6
What goes missing when Wallace is testing the Bully Proof Vest?

Q12 What coin operated contraption helps to prepare dinner?

Q13 What costume must Gromit wear for the Snoozatron?

Question 14
Which of Wallace's creations share his love for crackers?

Q7 What happens when the vest is activated?

Q15 How does Gromit stop this unruly invention?

Q8 What has prevented Wallace from falling asleep?

Q9 What purpose does the Tellyscope serve?

YOUR SCORE
....../15

BLUEPRINT

MOON ROCKET | MISSION: TO FIND CHEESE

RIVETS

CONTROL MECHA

WALLPAPER

CREW

BOARDING LADDER

PROPOSED TAKE OFF FROM CONSTRUCTION AREA (BASEMENT)

GARDEN

SECRET

42

THE HOUSE NEXT DOOR

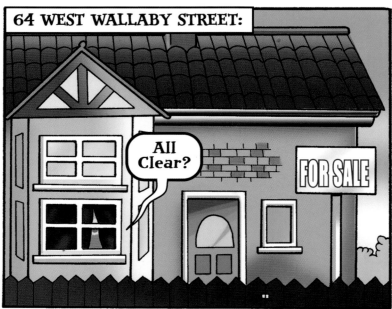

All Clear?

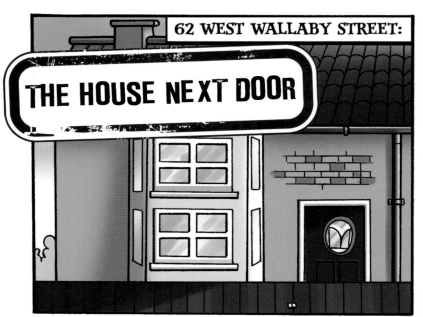

Looks like it, *Ena.* No sign of life, anyhow.

Good. They'll be here soon. If we're lucky, we can get 'em in and out without anyone being any the wiser. And then...

...*Le Costa Packet,* here we come!

Just think, *Arthur*... no more *mini-earthquakes* in the middle of the night!

No more *sub-orbital* sausages come barbecue season!

No more *projectile* paint when he's decorating!

Just sun, sea...

"... and *normal* next-door neighbours!"

SHORTLY...

Come in, come in. You'd be Mister and Mrs Collander, right?

That's us. *Reg* and *Pat*. Fine lookin' place you've got here.

Oh yes. Lovely. Nice and bright. I think it'd suit us down to the ground. What d'you think, Reg?

Aye, best we've seen so far, right enough.

AND SO...

Quiet neighbourhood?

Ah, mm, fair to middling, I'd say.

Ooo... lovely.

I think the missus 'as already set 'er heart on movin' in. We'll have a chat with the estate agent and—

KRAASHH!

What's *happening?*

What the-?

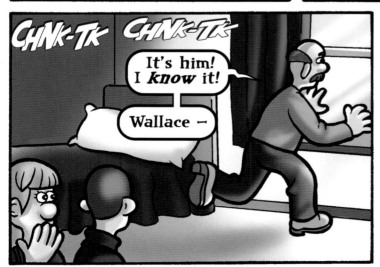

CHNK-TK CHNK-TK

It's him! I *know* it!

Wallace —

— what are you-? *Hh!*

Sorry, Arthur...

THE NEXT DAY...

As you can see, all mod cons. Plumbing's in tip top condition. Checked it all meself.

Yes, so I can see. It's...

... er, making a *funny* noise?

TKTA

TKTA

KUUUSH!

Eek!

SPOW

FLUUSH!

THRRP

Reg, what is it? What's happenin' to me beautiful bathroom?!

It's him! Who else?

Wallace!

Waaallace!

And... we're done. Trust me...

...you won't *recognize* the place!

Ay up?

Crikey!

Well I'll be—

Well I never—

Job well done, Gromit. Still, I'll miss Arthur and Ena. Been good neighbours, they have. What is it now... fifteen years? More?

Wallace — wait!

We like what you've done to the house so much...

...we're *staying!*

DUN-ROAMIN'!

51

SHOPPER 13

Fed up with the weekly trip to the shops? Well, Wallace has come up with a contraption which boldly goes where no shopping trolley has gone before.

Deep beneath 62 West Wallaby Street, Wallace and Gromit prepare to launch their latest invention.

Wallace hits the ignition, and from underground there emerges a remote-controlled shopping trolley which trundles forth on its thirteenth mission.

With Wallace reading out directions from a map book, Gromit wrestles with a series of levers to guide the trolley towards its destination...

... the local Pick 'N' Save! The trolley's built-in camera scans the shelves until it finds just what Wallace is looking for – the biggest cheese in the store.

But the weight of the giant Edam makes one of the wheels come off the trolley. "Gromit, we have a problem," announces a worried Wallace.

The trolley spins around in lopsided circles, until Gromit manages to make it grab a baguette which it uses as a crutch to support itself.

As Wallace stares at his cheese-less crackers, Gromit follows the progress of the intrepid trolley on screen as it makes its way home.

As it rolls through the local park, disaster is narrowly avoided as a football bounces in front of it like an out-of-control meteor.

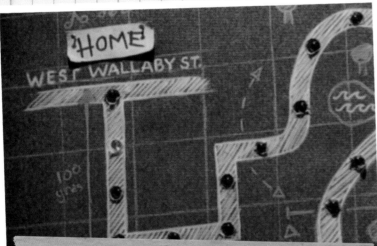

But Gromit manages to steer it through every obstacle, and soon Shopper 13 is ready to re-enter 62 West Wallaby Street.

But at the last moment tragedy strikes! The other wheel comes off the trolley and the giant Edam rolls back down the garden path.

"The Edam is stranded," moans Wallace. "We'll have to launch the probe!" And right on cue, Shaun the Sheep shoots out of a cat-flap in the garage door, riding on a skateboard.

But the rescue mission fails to go to plan, as a horrified Wallace sees Shaun start to tuck into a tasty cheese feast!

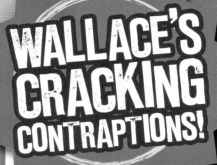

THE 525 CRACKERVAC

Wallace plans to introduce some sweeping changes with his latest invention, but it's Gromit who ends up trying to tame an unruly vacuum cleaner.

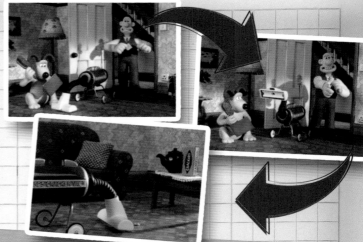

It's a dog's life for Gromit as he sweeps up some cracker crumbs Wallace has dropped on the floor. But before he can finish, a strange contraption rushes in and does the job for him.

Wallace proudly introduces him to the 525 Crackervac – a mobile vacuum cleaner with a built-in cracker sensor which can detect the tiniest crumb on the carpet.

But unfortunately its sensor is a bit too strong, and no sooner has it sucked up the crumbs than it picks up the scent of some other crackers nearby.

As the Crackervac lunges for the full pack of crackers on the table, Wallace tries to intervene – "Oi! Gerroff!"

He grabs the other end of the packet and a tug of war ensues. "Gromit! It's gone crackers!" he cries, as he tries to free the packet from the gnashing teeth of his creation.

Managing to wrestle it free, Wallace takes hasty action to get rid of the evidence: "Here, catch!" he shouts, throwing them to Gromit.

With a sinister growl, the Crackervac turns its attentions to Gromit, who raises his ears, ready for action.

Gromit narrows his eyes and the Crackervac gives a menacing stare – it's going to be High Noon for one of them!

Cool as a cucumber, Gromit takes a cracker from the packet, twirls it in his paw and then throws it high into the air...

... And as the distracted vacuum cleaner stretches out to grab the flying snack, Gromit twirls a rope, lassos it by the neck and rides it like a bucking bronco.

Gromit finally manages to subdue the household horror, tying a knot in its neck. But this drastic action makes its bag explode...

... Covering Wallace in a shower of dirt. "Eurgh Gromit!" he coughs. "I think you'd better get the dustpan and brush!"

WHERE BEAGLES DARE

Morning Wallace!

Morning, Mrs. tinkle! I'm here for little Prince's *walkies!*

YAP YAP YAP YAP

Ah, *there's* the little fellow! Hullo!

YAP YAP YAP

Are you sure I can't give you any *money* for this?

Ooh no, Mrs. Tinkle - I wouldn't *dream* of asking for anything!

Old Gromit over there - he just *loves* walking these dogs! Just look at his *happy little face!*

If you're sure? Then you make sure he gets a nice, long run!

Oh, I can *guarantee* that!

Come along Gromit, stop mucking about - time for *walkies.*

Let's take these little fellows to the *basement.*

Look at the lights! Soon this dynamo will produce enough electricity that we won't have to pay the electricity bills for a *month!*

MROWL?

CLOTHE-O-MATIC

KER-CHUNK

And with a click of the old *clothe-o-matic,* altered for this occasion --

CLOTHE-O-MATIC

-- Instant *postie* to chase!

And, if they don't like chasing postmen --

WHOOSH

WHOOSH

CLOTHE-O-MATIC

FETCH!

YAP

YAP YAP

-- What could *possibly* go wrong!

PLINK

Well *done*, Gromit!

SNIP

LATER.

Right then - I'll take the cat next door while you round up the dogs - I think they've had *enough*, don't you?

TEN DOG RETURNS LATER...

Thank you Wallace! Oh he *does* look like he's had a good run!

You've done a *grand* job! Same time tomorrow?

Oh *no*, Mrs. Tinkle --

-- I've had enough of *walkies* for a while!

END

MAKE YOUR OWN...
...LISTENING IN DEVICE!

TIMESCALE

WANT TO LISTEN IN TO SECRET DISCUSSIONS FROM A DISTANCE? FANCY SEEING IF SOMEONE IS SPEAKING ABOUT YOU BEHIND YOUR BACK? HERE'S HOW...

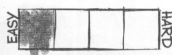

EASY — HARD

How to do it:

1. Wash out two empty yoghurt pots after dinner one evening and leave them overnight to dry.

2. Take your piece of string, preferably as long as you can make it, and tie a knot in both ends of it.

3. Now all you have to do is fix each end of the string to a yoghurt pot by Sellotaping the knots to the bottom of each pot. Make sure the string is firmly attached, otherwise this could jeopardise your secret mission!

4. Place one end of the device in a discreet position, where you will pick up conversation, and then take the other pot to a secret location where you can listen in!

5. You can even decorate your pots so they're camouflaged!

What you will need:
- Two yoghurt pots
- Sellotape
- String

YOGHURT POT

KNOT

THE STRING NEEDS TO BE KEPT TAUT TO WORK

HAVE YOU GOT A NEED FOR SPEED? RACE THIS LITTLE CONTRAPTION AROUND YOUR HOUSE AT WILL!

EASY — HARD

What you will need:

- Cotton Reel
- Thick corrugated cardboard
- Cocktail stick
- Pencil
- Elastic band
- Scissors
- Pencil

How to do it:

1. Cut two small circles from your cardboard, so to fit either end of your cotton reel, and cut through a small hole in the middle of each piece – big enough to fit an elastic band through.

2. Take your cotton reel and place your pieces of cardboard on either end. Push the elastic band through the reel and the hole in the cardboard.

3. Break the cocktail stick in two and place one piece between the elastic band and a circle of cardboard. Put the pencil in the same place at the other end of the reel.

4. To make your tank go, turn the pencil to tighten the band. This builds up energy to accelerate.

5. Put the tank on the floor with the pencil touching the ground and let go. Your tank will move best on smooth surfaces.

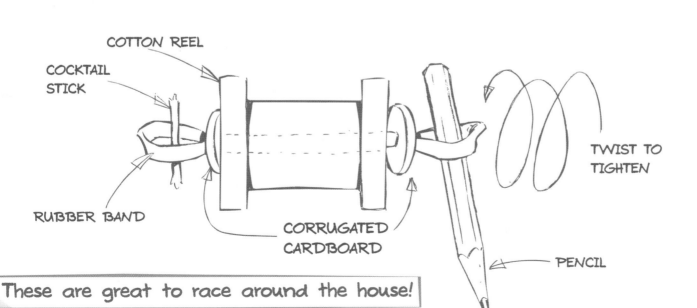

COTTON REEL

COCKTAIL STICK

TWIST TO TIGHTEN

RUBBER BAND

CORRUGATED CARDBOARD

PENCIL

These are great to race around the house!

67

...PENNY CLEANER!

TIMESCALE

TURN YOUR DULL, DARK PENNIES INTO SUPER SHINY COINS!

EASY — HARD

VINEGAR

SALT

What you will need:

- Some old, dull pennies!
- 1/4 cup white vinegar
- 1 teaspoon salt
- A shallow plastic bowl (not metal)
- Water

How to do it:

1. Pour the salt and vinegar into the bowl, stirring until the salt dissolves.

2. Take one penny and hold it in the liquid for ten seconds. What happens?

3. Now place the rest of your pennies into the bowl and watch as they are cleaned! Leave your pennies in the liquid for five minutes before removing and drying.

Now you should have a collection of ultra clean pennies!

OLD PENNIES

You can re-do this experiment using lemon juice instead of vinegar if you wish.

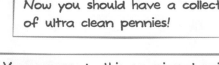

How does it work?

The reason pennies are so dull, usually, is because the copper they are made from slowly reacts with air in our atmosphere to form copper oxide. Pure copper is bright and shiny, as you'll see with your new super clean pennies, but when it reaches a copper oxide state it becomes dull. In this experiment, the acetic acid in the vinegar helps to dissolve the copper oxide, restoring them back to their shiny state and leaving the dulling copper in the liquid!

...BATTERY TESTER!

TIMESCALE

NEED TO FIND A NEW BATTERY FOR THE REMOTE CONTROL BEFORE YOUR FAVOURITE SHOW IS ON? OR FOR A TOY OR GAME? THE QUICKEST WAY TO FIND OUT IF YOUR SPARE BATTERIES ARE DUDS OR GOODS TO GO IS BY USING A BATTERY TESTER!

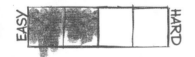

EASY ⬛⬛⬜⬜ HARD

What you will need:

- Bulb
- Bulb holder
- Two wires
- Battery

Note: You will need to buy a small bulb and holder from a hardware store, unless an adult happens to have one already!

How to do it:

1. Take your lightbulb and place it in its holder.

2. Connect the holder to the two wires and then onto the battery. If you are using a PP3 type battery, make sure you plug a wire onto each of the nodules (positive and negative). If you are using a standard AA or AAA battery, then you will need to hold the wires either side of the battery.

3. When you connect the wires to the battery - through whatever method is necessary - the bulb should light up if the battery is fully functional.

4. If it doesn't, your battery is a dud and won't help you change channel any quicker!

5. You can also use this set up to test if the bulb for your torch is working.

6. Simply use a battery that you know to work (testing it first with the bulb tester!) and replace the bulb in the equipment with the one you want to test.

7. If it lights up, then it will work in your room/torch, if it doesn't, throw it away!

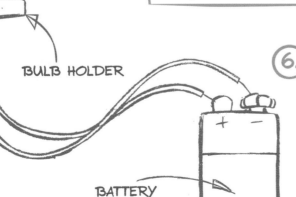

BULB

BULB HOLDER

WIRES

BATTERY

Wallace and Gromit's QUIZ! PART 3

TEST YOUR KNOWLEDGE OF WALLACE AND GROMIT'S ADVENTURES IN 'THE CURSE OF THE WERE-RABBIT'!

Question 1
What competition is approaching, offering the Golden Carrot Award as the prize?

Q2 What vegetable security and pest control service does Wallace set up to exploit the competition?

Q3 What happens when Wallace flicks the machine's switch from 'blow' to 'suck'?

Question 4
What do they name this rabbit?

70

Q5 What does Wallace's Mind-O-Matic do to the rabbits'?

Q6 Who is Wallace's rival?

Q7 Why does he want to capture the Were-Rabbit?

Question 8
What are the only things capable of killing the Were-Rabbit?

Question 9
Who does Wallace believe to be the Were-Rabbit?

Q10 Who is actually the Were-Rabbit

Q11 What does Gromit use to try and distract the Were-Rabbit when it breaks into the vegetable contest?

Q12 What does Gromit put on to try and protect the Were-Rabbit?

Q13 Who is Gromit's canine rival?

Q14 What cheese is used to revive Wallace?

Q15 What giant vegetable is used to try and trap the Were-Rabbit?

YOUR SCORE
...../15

Wallace and Gromit's Quiz! PART 4

OUR TWO HEROES HAVE ENCOUNTERED A WIDE ARRAY OF CHARACTERS IN THEIR JOURNEYS, HOW WELL DO YOU REMEMBER THE MOST PROMINENT PERSONALITIES?

Question 1
What brand of bread did Piella Bakewell appear in the commercials for?

Q2 What were Wallace and Gromit doing when they first met this pair?

Q3 What is the name of her pet dog?

Q4 Wallace believes that he and Wendoelene are made for each other when he discovers that her father did what as a profession?

Q5 Her dog, Preston, Is not a normal dog. How so?

Q6 What is Wendolene's profession?

Q7 What is Lady Tottington's first name?

Q8 Where does she live?

Q13 Who developed the Techno Trousers before Wallace got his hands on them?

Question 9
What is the name of the local policeman in Wallace's village?

Q14 What character do Wallace and Gromit meet on the moon?

WALLACE'S KNIT-O-MATIC

Q10 What is the name given to the sheep adopted by Wallace and Gromit after it has been sucked into the Knit-O-Matic?

Q15 What souvenir does Wallace source from this unusual character?

Q11 What does the vicar use to protect himself from the Were-Rabbit?

Q12 What animal did many believe criminal mastermind Feathers McGraw to be originally?

YOUR SCORE
......./15

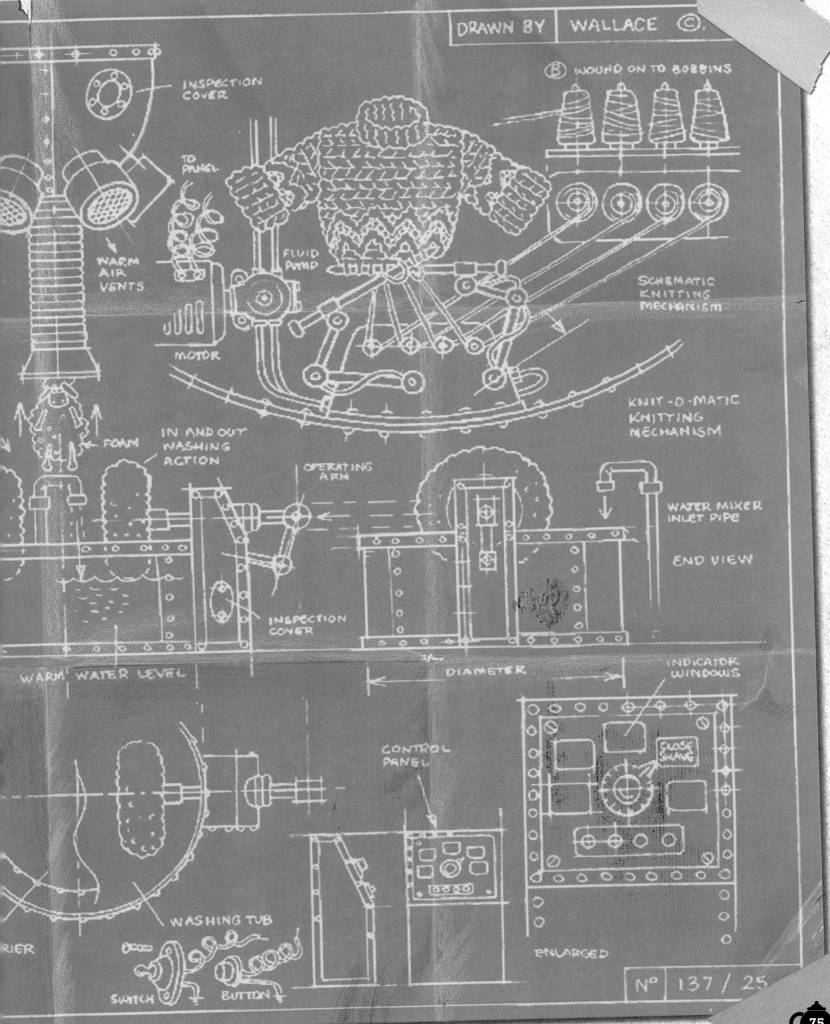

WASHDAY BLUES

Another culinary masterwork, lad. Whatever you're doing with those potatoes, they're more delicious than ever.

RUMMMMBLE

Gromit -- you haven't been using the washing machine to... er, *soften the produce,* have you?

CRRRREEEAAAKK

CRUNNNCH

GLUG GLUG GLUG GLUG

SPLOOOSH

Oh dear!

...No good, lad. Meteor say it'll be three weeks until they can get us a replacement. There's only one thing for it ...

Good for... scale models, eh?

SUD'S LAW

WASH & DRY

Well, we've been needing some extra curtains...

Now this is just *ridiculous!*

THE POWDER KEG

We can't be having this, lad. It's time we faced facts. We're going to have to...

We might be down to our last pairs of underpants, Gromit, but have no fear. My latest invention is going to *revolutionise* the laundry process.

No more searching for un-paired socks! No more tedious sorting, drying, folding and ironing! Ladies, gentlemen, dogs --

I give you -- the *Inspinerator!*

《《Ready for laundry》》

《《All scanners activated. Please insert powder and maintain a safe distance》》

Choo!

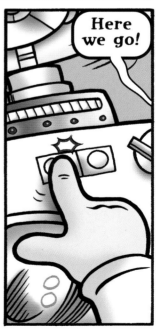

Here we go!

《Laundry detected. Soil level: barely worn. Response: rapid wash, light spin》

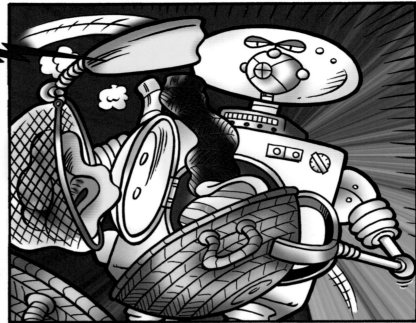

VOOSH VOOSH VOOSH

CLANK CLANK

VMMMM

ZRRR ZRRR ZRRR

FLUMPH

A friendly fellow, who takes all the hardship out of staying clean!

Now! That's enough of that!

JER UNKKH

Ohhhhh! Now I know how the socks feel!

《Error! Error! Please run diagnostic, reinstall drivers and press any key to resta-- ✱✱✱》

《-AARR-》

《-RR-》

Perhaps somebody has a spare... coat? *Anyone?*

HERE IS THE NUDES!

INVENTOR MAKES GREAT EXHIBITION!

WASHING CLOTHES BY HAND! TRADITION'S NOT ALWAYS BAD!

WASHING MACHINE TAKES POWER NAP!

SUDS' LAW

SCREEEK EEK EEK

Not much that can go wrong when you're using the old *elbow grease,* eh, lad?

I'd rather not air our *dirty laundry* in public again. The only washing-related press I want to make in the foreseeable future is for *trousers.*

But I'm sure we can put a *positive spin* on this little misunderstanding; get back to normal.

Besides, it'll all come out in the wash, eh?

Eh?

END CYCLE, DRAIN.

THE AUTOCHEF

Never one to rest on his laurels, Wallace has come up with a new invention guaranteed to make breakfast go with a bang!

"I think I've cracked it this time," announces Wallace as he tinkers with a remote control at the breakfast table one morning.

But Gromit has seen enough of his master's experiments to know that now is the time to reach for his waterproofs.

Wallace prods away at the buttons on the remote: "Two full English breakfasts coming up..." he chuckles.

His new invention, the Autochef, trundles into the dining room, greeting them with a mechanical "Top of the morning".

"Scrambled eggs, eh lad?" suggests Wallace, as he pushes the appropriate button on the remote.

"Grubs up!" says the Autochef after a few moments' whirring – and the eggs are quite literally up as they fly out of the blender and all over Gromit.

"Bon appétit!" barks the Autochef, as Wallace selects the Fried Egg option on the remote.

And the Autochef delivers two eggs sunny side up – right over Wallace's eyes, blinding him momentarily.

Wallace's tinkering doesn't seem to have ironed out all the bugs in the Autochef, as it starts to squirt tea at Gromit.

Gromit grabs a handy banana skin and sticks it over the Autochef's spout, which sends the machine into a frenzy.

Emitting a stream of bizarre robotic phrases, the Autochef finally announces 'Knickers' and promptly explodes.

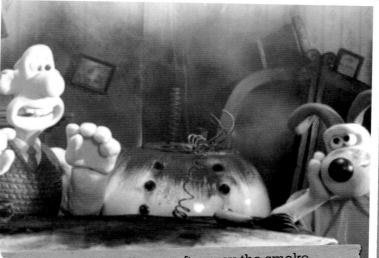

A crestfallen Wallace wafts away the smoke and announces: "I think I'll have the continental tomorrow, lad."

WALLACE'S CRACKING CONTRAPTIONS!

THE TURBO DINER

Wallace's plans for a slap-up meal turn into pure slapstick, as Gromit has to "guess what's coming to dinner!"

It's nearly time for tea, and as usual Wallace has left the dining table in a complete mess. Gromit sighs as he starts to clear things away...

... Only to be interrupted by Wallace, excitedly introducing his latest invention: "My new Turbo Diner will take care of everything!"

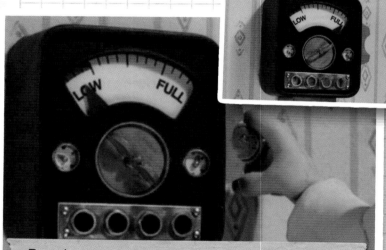

Popping a coin into the electricity meter, Wallace flicks a switch and sets his contraption whirring into life.

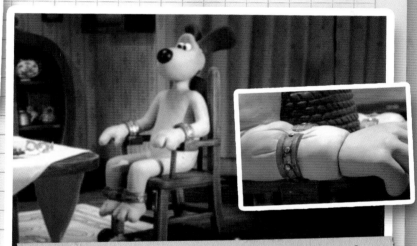

Seating themselves at the table, Wallace and Gromit find their arms and legs automatically clamped to the chairs.

A giant vacuum cleaner drops down from the ceiling and starts to suck up the mess. "That's 300 horsepower of pure suck!" chuckles Wallace.

So strong is the force of the suction that it's only the clamps which stop Wallace and Gromit being sucked up too.

Then another compartment drops down with a clunk. Gromit looks on nervously as the machine whirrs into life again...

But for once, it looks like Wallace has got things right! The compartment heads back into the ceiling, leaving a sumptuous dinner behind.

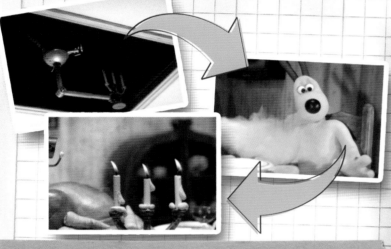

And as the piece de resistance, a flame-thrower drops down and lights the candles – if a little too enthusiastically...

But just as Gromit is ready for the perfect meal, the meter runs out – leaving the pair clamped to their chairs and unable to stick in any more coins.

The dinner-less duo exchange awkward glances as they look at the delicious feast they are unable to enjoy.

And then the lights go out, leaving the room lit just by candles. "Lovely atmosphere anyway, eh?" says the ever-optimistic Wallace.

BAA-KING MAD

Gromit — come quick! It's *Shaun*...

He's only gone and polished off me blooming *Begonias!*

And the *Potpourri!*

He'll eat us out of home *and* garden at this rate. Only one thing for it.

Get the door, will you, Gromit...

VZZZ

TSHH!

It's the *basement* for you, me lad!

Let's see you find anything to ingest *down there!*

BAAA!

LATER...

I tell you, lad, there's **nothing** on the box these days. Think I'll finish up my cocoa and then turn in.

Want to be fully rested for the first test of the new, upgraded **mind-manipulation-o-matic** tomorrow.

I'm a nobody...

Hmm. Maybe I was too **hard** on Shaun? After all, he can't help himself. Only doing what comes naturally, eh lad?

Mm. Perhaps you're right. One night in the basement won't hurt him. Might even teach him a **lesson,** I suppose...

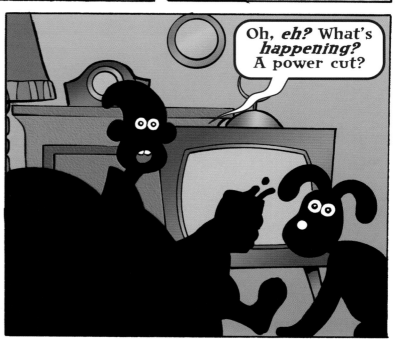

Oh, **eh?** What's **happening?** A power cut?

Hang on... **no,** can't be. The streetlights are all still on. Must've blown a fuse somewhere.

Sort it out will you, Gromit? I'm off to bed...

93

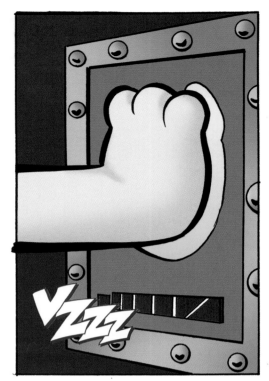

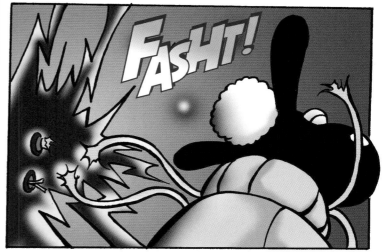

TSHH

VZZZ

KLKT

CHOMP

KER LANK
KER LANK

EEENK!

Gromit, what's all this noise about?

Gromit?

Who's there? Grom—

CHOMP

SOON...

Well, I've repaired the damage...

Soon have you both the *right way around.*

I hope.

Well?

BAAA!

THE NEXT DAY...

All's well that ends well, eh lad? And at least we know the new mind-manipulation-o-matic does the trick!

Any *after* effects?

No? Good, good. I'll give it a proper test later, when *Wendolene* and the vicar pop in for tea.

CRNCH

Gromit?

Gromit!

THE BLOOMIN' END!

...ULTIMATE PAPER PLANE!

TIMESCALE

EASY | | | | HARD

BE THE ENVY OF ALL YOUR FRIENDS WITH THIS SUPER SMOOTH FLYER, WHICH SOARS ELEGANTLY THROUGH THE AIR AND CAN BE DESIGNED TO YOUR DESIRE!

What you will need:
- Sheet of paper
- Some colouring pencils

How to do it:

(1.) Fold the sheet of paper in half, width ways.

(2.) Fold the corners to the centre of the page.

(3.) Fold to the centre again.

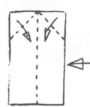

(4.) Fold in half again.

(5.) Fold out wings.

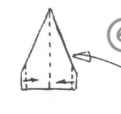

(6.) Fold the two corners of the plane behind the wings and allow to drop down - leaving them hanging downwards adjacent to the middle of the plane, to aid flight.

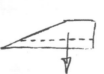

(7.) Decorate in your own style.

(8.) Go flying!

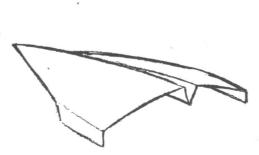

100

...HELICOPTER!

TIMESCALE

FANCY SOMETHING DIFFERENT? OUT-DO YOUR FRIENDS' PAPER PLANES BY MAKING A PAPER HELICOPTER!

EASY | | | | | HARD

What you will need:

- Sheet of paper

- Some colouring pencils

How to do it:

1. Using the template below, trace the design onto a piece of paper and cut out.

2. Fold horizontally along the dotted line at the top, cut down the solid line in the middle (folding the two flaps both ways) and roll up the bottom of the template to weigh down the helicopter.

3. Now you can drop your helicopter and see its propellers in action!

You can also experiment with making larger helicopters, but beware that the bigger you make it, the higher you'll have to drop it from.

...WATER BOMB!

TIMESCALE

ORGANISED A WATER FIGHT? ADD TO YOUR ARTILLERY WITH THIS GRENADE-LIKE WATER BOMB PERFECT TO AMBUSH YOUR FOES!

EASY ▯▯▯▯ HARD

How to do it:

What you will need:
- Sheet of paper
- Water

1. Take a piece of A4 paper and turn it into a square by folding a corner down to the edge and ripping off the excess paper.

2. Fold the newly formed square in half. Open it out and fold diagonally, one corner to the other. Open the paper and repeat for the other diagonal.

3. With the paper open and flat, fold it in half along the horizontal line. Push the corners inside the folded paper, along the folded lines from step two, and flatten the shape by running your finger over all of the creases.
You should be left with a triangle shape that has four flaps.

4. Place the paper in front of you with the longest edge nearest. Fold the two closest corners up to the top point of the shape and then repeat on the other side. Now you will have a diamond shape, with a opening on each side of the bomb!

5. Fold both corners of the diamond toward the centre on both sides, which will create pockets. Fold the flaps at the bottom of the bomb into the pockets.

6. Open up the bomb so it forms an 'X' shape. Blow into the hole at the top of the bomb and blow into it so the paper balloons out, ready to be filled with water!

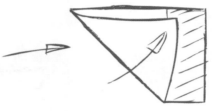

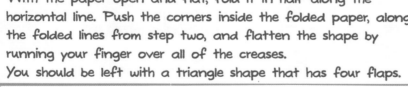
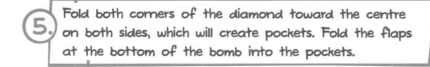

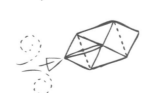

...LEMONADE!

TIMESCALE

AFTER SOAKING YOUR FRIENDS, BROTHERS AND SISTERS OR PARENTS, MAKE IT UP TO THEM BY MAKING A NICE REFRESHING GLASS OF HOMEMADE LEMONADE!.

EASY ◼◻◻◻ HARD

What you will need:

- Some lemons (depending on how many people you're making for)
- Sugar
- Baking soda
- Water
- Cups or glasses

How to do it:

1. Squeeze the juice from a lemon into a glass.

2. Then add water - making sure that you have an equal amount of lemon juice to water.

3. Add a teaspoon of baking soda to your concoction and mix well.

4. Sprinkle a little sugar in, too, and mix, this will give it a sweet taste.

5. Try some of your lemonade, adding a little more sugar if you think it should be sweeter, and there you have it - a glass of lemonade!

TEASPOON OF BAKING SODA

SPRINKLE A LITTLE SUGAR TO TASTE

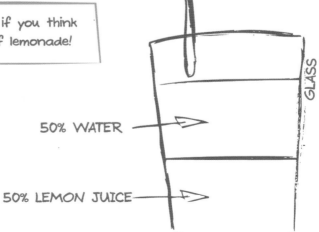

GLASS

50% WATER

50% LEMON JUICE

Repeat for as many people as you need.

Wallace and Gromit's Quiz!  PART 5

HOW WELL DO YOU KNOW WALLACE? THIS QUIZ FOCUSES ON OUR FAVOURITE WACKY INVENTOR!

Q1 What colour pullover does Wallace usually wear?

Q2 And what colour tie?

Q3 What is his favourite food?

Q4 And his favourite type of that food?

Q5 Which of Wallace's girlfriends was allergic to cheese?

Q6 By which nickname did Wallace refer to Lady Tottington?

Q7 What does his 'Dough to Door' service in 'A Matter of Loaf and Death' offer?

Q8 What sort of business does Wallace start in 'A Close Shave'?

Q9 And in 'The Curse of the Were-Rabbit'?

Q10 Who was Wallace engaged to in 'A Matter of Loaf and Death'?

Question 11
What was Piella's secret?

Q12 How does his fiancée die?

Q13 In 'The Wrong Trousers', how does Wallace pay off his debts?

Q14 What magazine can Wallace sometimes be found reading?

Q15 What type of cheese does Wallace sample in 'A Grand Day Out'?

YOUR SCORE
....../15

DRAWING Nº 230

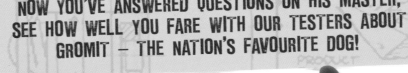

Wallace and Gromit's QUIZ! PART 6

NOW YOU'VE ANSWERED QUESTIONS ON HIS MASTER, SEE HOW WELL YOU FARE WITH OUR TESTERS ABOUT GROMIT – THE NATION'S FAVOURITE DOG!

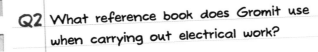

Q2 What reference book does Gromit use when carrying out electrical work?

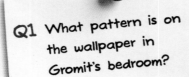

Q1 What pattern is on the wallpaper in Gromit's bedroom?

Q3 Who is Gromit's favourite Russian novelist?

Q4 What classic composer does Gromit occasionally listen to?

Q5 In 'A Grand Day Out', what does Gromit do to allow Wallace's moon rocket to take off?

Q6 What does Gromit prevent Feathers McGraw from stealing in 'The Wrong Trousers'?

Q7 What chase ensues before the penguin is stopped?

Q8 What sheep does Gromit befriend in 'A Close Shave'?

Question 9
What evil dog do the duo help to destroy in the same film?

Q10 Who is Gromit's girlfriend in 'A Matter of Loaf and Death'?

Q11 What is the couple's favourite song?

Q12 In 'The Curse of the Were-Rabbit', what rabbit do Wallace and Gromit adopt?

Q13 Who captures Gromit in that film?

Q14 Which contraption does Gromit have to drive to the shops?

Q15 What fruit does Gromit use to stop the haywire Auto Chef?

YOUR SCORE ...../15

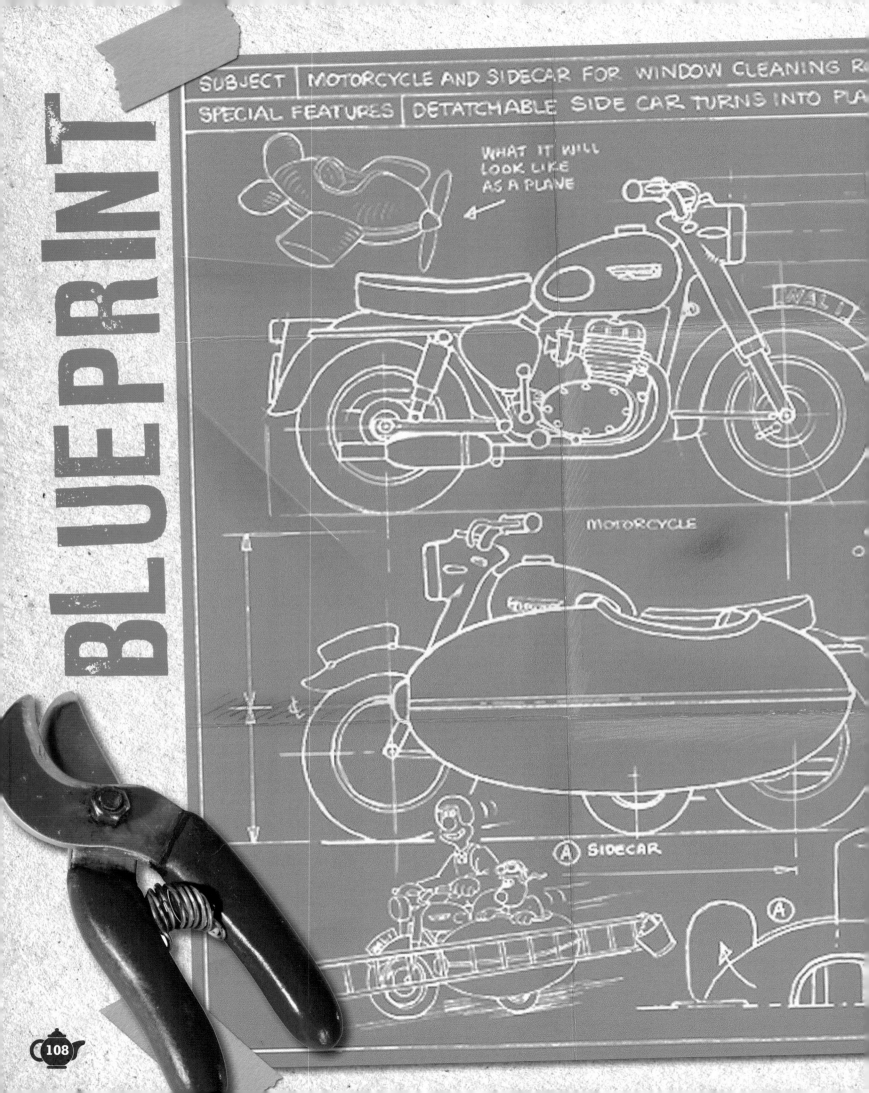

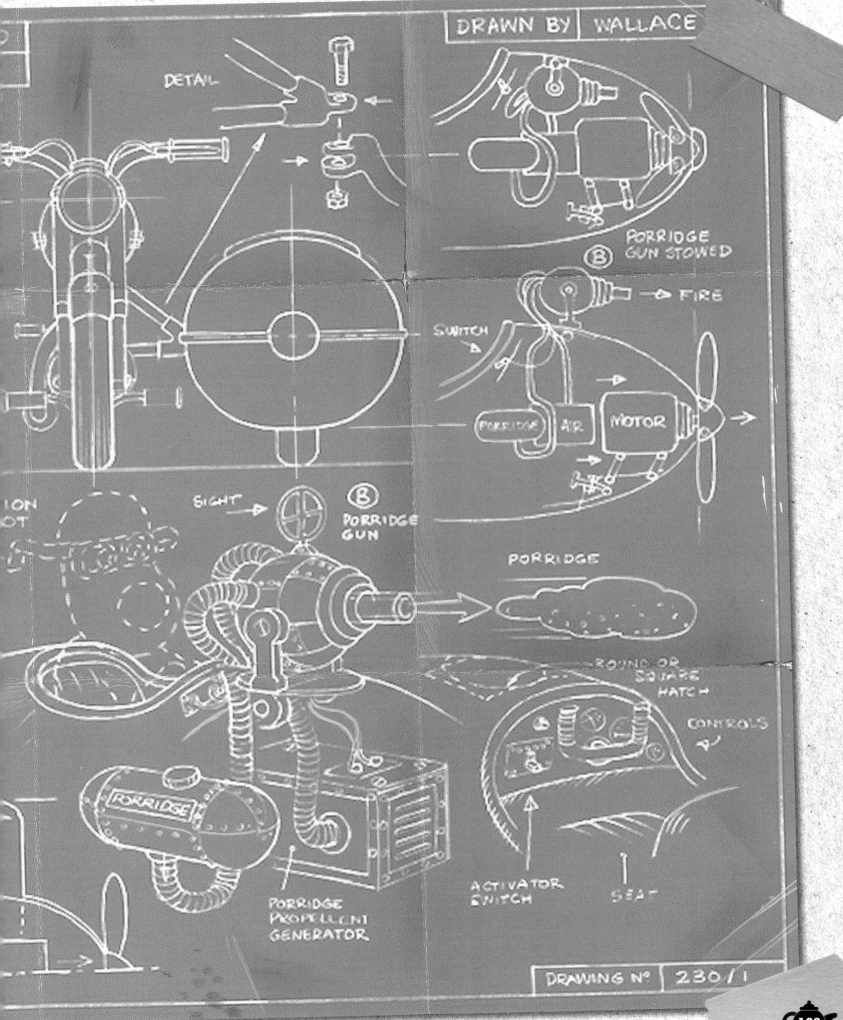

DETAIL

PORRIDGE
Ⓑ GUN STOWED

FIRE

SWITCH

PORRIDGE AIR MOTOR

SIGHT → Ⓑ PORRIDGE GUN

ION OT

PORRIDGE

ROUND OR SQUARE HATCH

CONTROLS

PORRIDGE

PORRIDGE PROPELLENT GENERATOR

ACTIVATOR SWITCH

SEAT

A SHARP IDEA

...and, it occurred to me that I spend a lot of time not *actually inventing* at all...

...just *sharpening pencils* so that I *can* invent.

In fact, I lose *3.7 days a year* sharpening my pencils. Can you believe that, Gromit?

Actually it's 3.6931778-something-something days, but I rounded it up to give you an *idea* of the amount of *loss* we're talking about.

Although, do you think I might have *carried a three* here where I shouldn't have?

You wouldn't mind *double-checking* my figures, when you get a *moment,* eh, lad?

Anyway, *the point* is...

... well, actually that is *the point,* isn't it? The *pencil point,* do you see, Gromit? Heh-heh.

And so, I have *built* us...

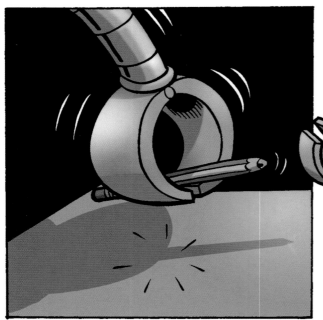

COMMENCING SECONDARY SHARPENING LEVEL.

WHRRRRR

THE NEXT MORNING...

Hurry up, Gromit -- my *eggs* are *nearly* ready!

DAIRY

WEST WALLABY STREET

Mmmm, it's *no good* having eggs for *breakfast* without some nice *bread* to go with them, is it?
I don't know what we'd do without our *morning delivery* from the *baker's.*

Instantly toasted to *perfection, crispy* on the outside and *fluffy* in the mid-...

HANG ON!

WAK WAK WAK WAK WAK

Something's *not right* here. Have you been *pruning* the garden again, lad?

Eh? Something's *definitely* wrong here.

Mrs Roberts at number 68 could *never* manage to do *that* to *her garden*, not with the way her *arthritis* has been playing her up.

Look *sharp*, lad -- we have work to do!

SOON...

Crikey! It's *worse* than I thought...

CHEZ WIG

C. Atkinso Ltd

...and yet it's all so random and *pointless!* Or is it...?

THE FRATELLIS

Crikey, I think it's *spreading...*

HIYA   VODOZ   TOTTIES   2000 BC   NEERH   DOCTOR WHAT

CHEESE TIMES

SPORT   NARGIAN

BRITZ

SOU

AT'S HE OINT ?

WAL1

SCREECH

THE DAILY MAGNIFIER

...has Big Ben always been that *pointy?*

PARLIAMENT'S DOGGED PURSUIT FOR HIGHER WAGES

Never mind that now -- *whatever's* caused this has unwittingly *tipped* us off by leaving an *easy trail* to follow!

Come along, Gromit -- put that paper *down*, we're in the middle of a *high speed chase* here...

DOGGED PURSUIT

...have you no *sense of occasion?*

WHRRRRR

Really, lad, sometimes I *despair*, I really do.

What's that?

SMASHHH!

Waitaminute! What's my *robot sharpener* doing *out here?*

Didn't we *leave* it in the *cellar...?* It *shouldn't* be...

GOUD GOUDA

BEDDAR CHEDDAR

WHRRRRR

...sharpening *cheese?!!?*

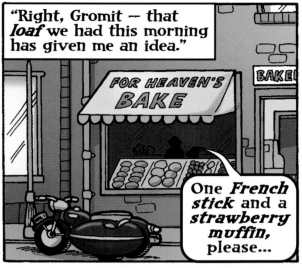

"Right, Gromit -- that *loaf* we had this morning has given me an idea."

One *French stick* and a *strawberry muffin*, please...

Ooh, and those *sausage rolls* look good, let's have a couple of those for me and the boy, too.

Well, lad, we've a lot to do -- it's *no good* working on an *empty stomach!*

Red, I think.

This *won't do*, Gromit - - the paint won't *dry* quickly enough!

Make sure you *bring it back* though -- Mrs *Tedder's* due for her *perm* at four-thirty!

THE OLD LADIES' HAIRDRESSER

Now, where's that *muffin?*

Perfect! Seems almost a *shame* to *waste,* after all that *hard work.*

WHRRRRR

♪

PUB

SHARPENING REQUIRED

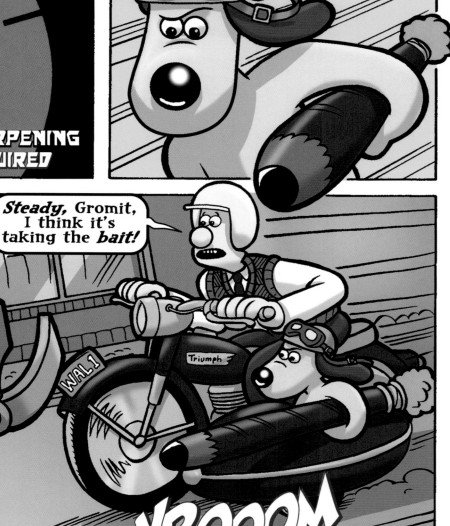

Steady, Gromit, I think it's taking the *bait!*

Triumph

WAL 1

VROOOM VROOOM

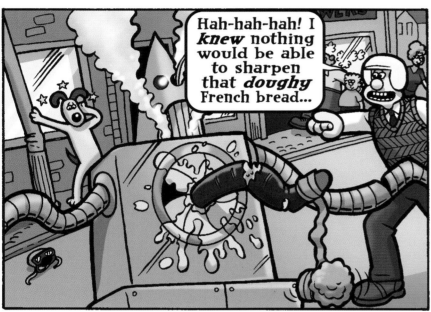

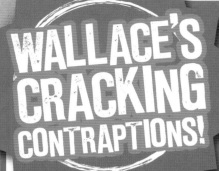

WALLACE'S CRACKING CONTRAPTIONS!

THE SOCCAMATIC

Determined to show off his soccer skills to a goal-keeping Gromit, Wallace forgets to keep his eye on the ball...

"You'll have to keep on your toes this week," Wallace warns Gromit as he jogs out onto the soccer pitch.

"Whay-hey!" he shouts as he kicks the ball towards the goal where Gromit stands guard. But the plucky pooch manages to get his paw to it just in time.

However much he tries to emulate his footballing heroes, Wallace just can't seem to get past Gromit's goal-saving expertise.

Frustrated at not being able to put a ball in the back of the net, Wallace tries another tack. "That's you warmed up..." he tells Gromit.

"Time to move up a division," continues Wallace as he heads off, leaving a puzzled Gromit standing in goal.

Gromit's ears shoot up in surprise as Wallace returns, and he hurls himself to the ground to avoid a volley of footballs coming towards him.

Such is the velocity of the balls powering towards the goal, they leave the fence behind it peppered with holes.

"All the goals, none of the fuss," gloats Wallace as he sits comfortably on top of his latest invention...

...The Socccamatic! Wallace sips his tea as he proudly looks down at his patented ball-firing device.

But when he looks up, Gromit has put on a helmet, goggles and gloves, and stands ready to take on all comers.

Wallace looks on astonished as, with the pull of a toggle, Gromit's jersey inflates to fill the entire goal – even his gloves expand to giant size.

Never one to admit defeat, Wallace produces a racket and ball. "Anyone for tennis, perchance?" he asks.

THE BULLYPROOF VEST

Wallace's new way to tackle intruders certainly packs a punch, as Gromit finds out the hard way.

123

One dark and stormy night, Wallace is in the kitchen making himself a cuppa as the wind howls around outside.

The house seems full of eerie noises – creaking doors, strange caterwaulings and sinister footsteps – which leave Wallace feeling very nervous indeed.

As he makes his way back to the living room, Wallace is convinced he sees something moving out of the corner of his eye.

He peers fearfully towards the window, and when he looks back, the cracker in his hand has mysteriously disappeared.

With a nervous gulp, Wallace realises that there must be someone – or something – hiding in the wardrobe.

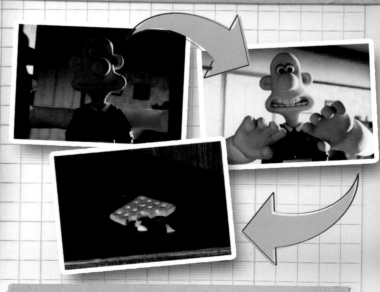

Summoning his courage, he flings the door back – but all he finds is a half-eaten cracker.

As he turns back, Wallace is confronted by the sight of Gromit dressed in a ninja outfit, twirling a rolling pin like some sort of martial arts weapon.

But Wallace is strangely confident at the sight of his attacker, and reaches for the button of a control panel on his tank-top.

A large boxing glove on a spring shoots out of his chest, sending Gromit sprawling across the room and seeing stars.

"Wha-hey! The Bullyproof Vest works like a treat!" crows Wallace as he switches the light on, revealing Gromit with a nasty black eye.

But in his delight, Wallace treads on the rolling pin and topples forward, just as the boxing glove shoots out of the Bullyproof Vest again…

…Sending him crashing into the ceiling. "You'd better get a ladder," groans Wallace. "I think I've cracked me artex!"

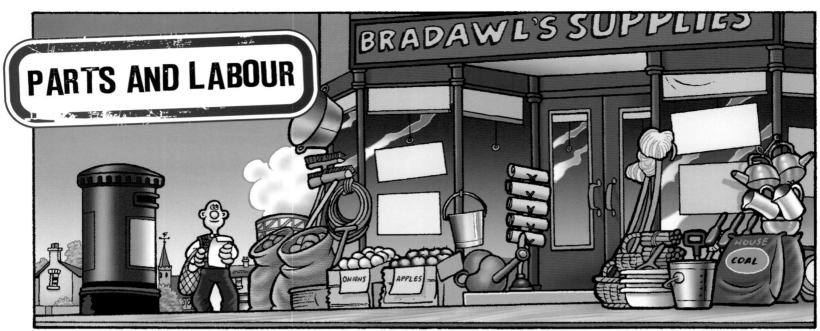

PARTS AND LABOUR

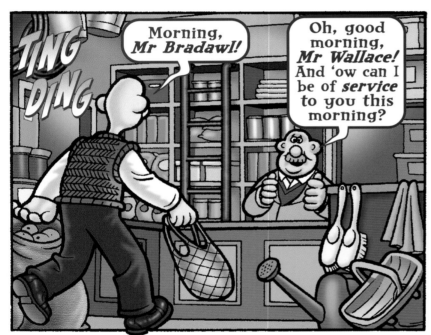

Morning, *Mr Bradawl!*

Oh, good morning, *Mr Wallace!* And 'ow can I be of *service* to you this morning?

Just a few items I'd like to pick up.

A box of three inch screws, a dozen rolls of gaffer tape, a can of red gloss paint...

Right you are.

Dibber! Make yourself useful, I say make yourself *useful!* A box of three inch screws for Mr Wallace!

Yes, Mr Bradawl, sir.

New help about the place?

Oh yes, that's Dibber. He's with me on *work opportunity*. Opportunity for sitting on his *backside,* if you ask me.

Now, what else?

Well, would you be stocking any pool scoops?

How many would you like?

Half a dozen?

126

SHORTLY...

Well, thanks again, Mr Bradawl. Good day to you!

TING DING

That were a right *odd* customer, Mr Bradawl. Six pool scoops? What'd he need those for?

Mr Wallace is a local inventor of great repute, Dibber. He often comes by to stock up on what we might regard as *'curious'* items...

...but which are *integral components,* I say integral components, of his latest project.

What is his latest project?

I... I don't know, lad. I've never asked. I don't like to pry.

LATER...

We'd best close up for the day, Dibber.

Yes, Mr Bradawl.

You've set me thinking, you know. I wonder what Mr Wallace was up to?

CLOSED

By gad, it must be a fine life, being an *inventor,* 'stead of stuck here in hardware retail, day in, day out.

It must be so fulfilling to be that *successful...*

CLOSED

TWO DAYS LATER...

TING DING

Morning, Mr Wallace! Nice to see you again, I say nice to see you! 'Ow can I help?

Oh, just a few items, Mr Bradawl. A four and three quarter inch locking piston, two counter-rotators and a metric bung measure.

Dibber! Customer!

We'll get you sorted right away, Mr Wallace. By the way, how did your last...uhm *project*... turn out?

Oh, that. Well, you might say it was a *runaway* success.

Excellent! I thought so.

Anything else on your list? Anything... *specialist?*

Well, I was wondering if you had any paddles. For canoes.

And any rubber sheeting, the kind from which one might fashion, say, a balloon?

Oh, I think I can help you there...

THREE DAYS LATER...

Mr Bradawl? There's...

...there's a *dog* here to see you.

Eh? Oh, that's *Gromit,* that is! Mr Wallace's dog.

How do, lad! Got a list for me have you? Good dog!

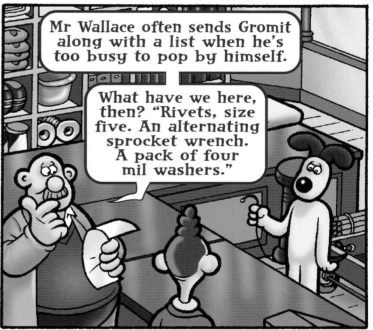

Mr Wallace often sends Gromit along with a list when he's too busy to pop by himself.

What have we here, then? "Rivets, size five. An alternating sprocket wrench. A pack of four mil washers."

We'll get right to it, I say we'll get to it. Put the items in the cart, Dibber.

Now what's this? "Heavy duty industrial springs, eight of?" I'll have to look out the back.

LATER...

Hey, Mr Bradawl, I found these washers on the counter.

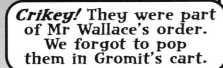

Crikey! They were part of Mr Wallace's order. We forgot to pop them in Gromit's cart.

By 'eck, these could be crucial, Dibber!

Crucial, Mr Bradawl?

Aye, *crucial* to the *success or failure* of Mr Wallace's next project!

'Ow would it be, I say 'ow would it be if, at the moment of truth, he reached round for a washer and there was none to be had?

Things could fall apart and what not!

Hold the fort, Dibber! I'm off to make a delivery!

But Mr Bradawl, I've only been here a week...

You've proved yourself to be a *fast learner,* I say a fast learner, son.

Now mind the shop while I complete this vital mission!

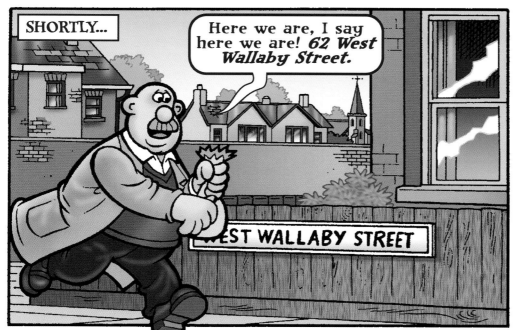

SHORTLY...

Here we are, I say here we are! *62 West Wallaby Street.*

WEST WALLABY STREET

By 'eck, I hope I'm in time to avert *catastrophe!*

RAP A TAP TAP

Mr Wallace? I say, Mr Wallace? It's Bradawl, from Bradawls! I've brought your washers!

Oooh! In here, Mr Bradawl!

Let yourself through!

You're just in time...

...to help me mend the sink.

GROMIT

Oh. *Sink?* Sink, is it? Not some... ...*amazing project?*

No, just the S-bend.

BEFORE LONG...

Well, I can't *thank* you enough, Mr Bradawl. *Very timely,* your arrival.

Don't mention it, I say don't mention it.

Perhaps I can offer you a cup of tea and a slice of cake by way of appreciation.

I won't say no.

So tell me, Mr Wallace, how's the *invention business?*

MAKE YOUR OWN...
...PHOTO FRAME!

THE PERFECT SENTIMENTAL PRESENT FOR A PARENT OR LOVED ONE, OR TO CELEBRATE ONE OF YOUR FAVOURITE MEMORIES.

How to do it:

EASY **■■■** HARD

What you will need:

- Old CD cases
- Scissors
- Glue
- Sticky tape
- Cardboard
- Decorative materials

1. Take an old CD case (with the permission of the owner, of course!) and remove the paper inserts and the plastic tray onto which the CD would usually sit.

2. Find the photo you would like to frame and cut it so it's just smaller than the empty plastic box you now have.

3. Stick your photo to the back of the box with some sticky tape (making sure that tape isn't visible through the plastic!).

4. Cut a piece of cardboard down to fit in the case too, and fix it into place behind the photo with sticky tape or glue. This will protect your photo.

5. Stand the case up so the front cover is face down, holding your image aloft. You can now put lines of glue around the outside cover to make a decorative margin and, if you're feeling extra creative, you can even decorate the back of the picture!

6. You can use things like beads, buttons, jelly beans, sequins, small toys, felt and other such matierals to create your decorative borders.

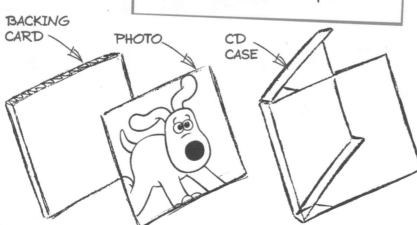

BACKING CARD   PHOTO   CD CASE

...PEN POT!

TIMESCALE

NEED SOMEWHERE TO PUT YOUR PENS AND PENCILS ON YOUR DESK? SOMEWHERE EASY TO GRAB THEM FROM? CREATE YOUR OWN, CUSTOMISED PENCIL AND PEN POT!

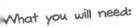

EASY — HARD

What you will need:

– Empty plastic container

– Drill

– Paper

– Glue

– Decorative materials

How to do it:

1. First of all, depending what was in the container previously, give it a good washing out and allow it to dry.

LID

2. Remove the container's lid (if it doesn't have a lid, you can skip this step) and ask an adult to help you drill various holes into it - this is where your pens and pencils will slot into, so make sure you're drilling holes wide enough to fit them into!

CONTAINER

DECORATIVE WRAP

3. Cut your piece of paper to fit the pot and wrap it round, ensuring it fits.

4. Before sticking it down with glue, decorate the paper how you wish with drawings. Once it has dried onto the pot, you can even stick further thing on top of your drawings to add to the design.

5. When satisfied with your creation, place on your desk and fill with pens and pencils. Now get on with some work!

FINISHED POT

137

MAKE YOUR OWN...

...SUBMARINE!

TIMESCALE

YOUR OWN UNDERWATER BOMBER, READY TO SEE OFF YOUR FOES! QUICK AND EASY TO MAKE, GREAT FUN TO PLAY WITH!

How to do it:

EASY  HARD

1. Cut two holes of equal diameter - around 4cm - into the bottle, one at the top, the other at the bottom. Do this on both sides, so the holes are opposing each other.

2. Put your tubing into your balloon, securing in place with Sellotape. Insert your spoons, or cutlery, through the nose to rest on the base of the bottle.

3. Now push the tubing (with balloon connected) through the nose of the bottle, so that the balloon part of the tubing is in the middle.

4. Now it's time to test your submarine out! Place into a sink or bathtub and fill with water until it covers your submarine. Blow into the end of the tubing and watch your sub whirr into action!

What you will need:

- Large plastic bottle (2 litre)
- Balloon
- Plastic tubing
- Four spoons
- Scissors
- Sellotape

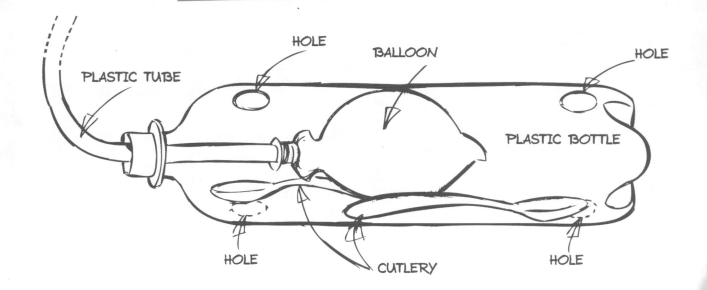

...INVISIBLE INK!

WANT TO WRITE A SECRET NOTE TO ONE OF YOUR FRIENDS WITHOUT ANYONE ELSE SPYING WHAT YOU'VE SAID? WE'VE GOT THE ANSWER FOR YOU...

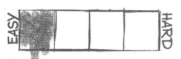

EASY | | | | HARD

What you will need:

- A carrot
- Lemon or lemon juice
- Paper
- Plate

How to do it:

1. With the help of a parent, sharpen your carrot so it is pointed at the end - this will be your pen!

2. Squeeze some lemon onto your plate. This will be your ink. For this you can either use something like Jif Lemon Juice, which is ready to go, or you can squeeze juice from a fresh lemon. You may need help from an adult to cut the lemon in half for this. Once that's done, just squeeze both halves of the lemon onto the plate.

3. Dip the tip of your carrot pen into the lemon juice and begin to write your letter. Remember to keep dipping your carrot in the juice, otherwise you will run out of ink!

4. Leave letter to dry and then give to the person you want to see it, telling them to put it in an airing cupboard (or against some other heat source) to reveal the secret message!

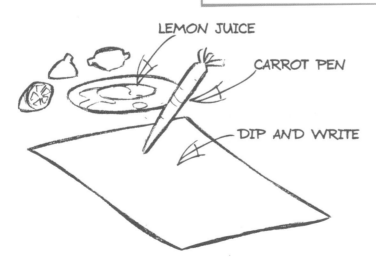

LEMON JUICE

CARROT PEN

DIP AND WRITE

HEAT SOURCE

Put the kettle on Gromit!

Did you know? - This technique was used by British spies during the Cold War!

ANSWERS

Page 13 - Easy Cheesy!

Page 12 - Mix & Match!

1. E   4. C
2. A   5. B
3. F   6. D

Page 16 - The Evening Post

Exclusive news reaching us here at The **E**vening Post suggests that there is a cake **t**hief in the area!

The sweet **t**oothe**d** crook is keen on **c**upcakes and **m**uffins, while he has also been linked to a spate of **b**iscuit thefts, too.

One victim was the local **b**aker, who came into work one morning to find all of his **i**ced **b**uns missing.

Speaking to our reporter, the baker said: "I am distraught, what will the people have for lunch now?"

Our advice would be to **l**ock up your **c**onfectionery and be on **g**uard at all times.

Page 17 - Easy Cheesy word search

```
C R O Q U E F O R T O  T O
H E W E N S L E Y G M
E C L Z Z O M P A O    R
L H B A Z Z A R Z R P  A
A E R P D M O Z Z G A  R
D D I A O F A R O O R  M
Y D A R V R V E M N    M
I D Z M E R B O L Z E
L R Z L D F L I D O Z
S R L L A Z O M A L Z
N A S E M R A P L A E
W E S E E H C N O O M
T R A D D E R S T I L
S T A Z E K L A B R S
S N O D S R A R R O T  T
Z T G R D M E P I Q    I
O E Y G E F A Z L U L  L
L L E O Z Q H Z O E M  M
A L O P A R M C M F O
M O S T I L T O N O P
```

Page 17 - Crossword

```
K
N E W S P A P E R
I       H     L       A
T       A     A       B
T       U     R       B
I       N     M       I
N             C       T
G             L
              B O N E
              C
              K
```

Page 17 - Sudoku

4	7	3	6	1	2	8	5	9
5	2	9	3	7	8	4	6	1
6	1	8	5	4	9	2	7	3
3	9	7	8	2	5	6	1	4
8	5	2	4	6	1	9	3	7
1	4	6	7	9	3	5	8	2
7	8	5	9	3	4	1	2	6
2	3	4	1	5	6	7	9	8
9	6	1	2	8	7	3	4	5

Page 38: Wallace and Gromit Quiz

1. A dog collar.
2. Techno Trousers.
3. The garage.
4. Because "everyone knows the moon is made out of cheese".
5. The Knit-O-Matic.
6. Shaun the Sheep.
7. Feathers McGraw.
8. Steal a diamond from the local museum.
9. The Cooker.
10. To ski.
11. Sleeping.
12. Preston.
13. Cheese.
14. Fluffles.

Page 40: Wallace and Gromit Quiz

1. The Christmas Cardomatic.
2. A Robin costume.
3. Scrambled Eggs.
4. A giant Edam cheese.
5. The Soccamatic.
6. A cracker.
7. A boxing glove shoots out of it.
8. Eating too much cheese.
9. Change TV channel without getting up.
10. A newspaper.
11. Wallace covered in snow.
12. The Turbo Diner.
13. A Sheep costume.
14. 525 Crackervac.
15. By lassoing it.

Page 70: Wallace and Gromit Quiz

1. Giant Vegetable Competition.
2. Anti-Pesto.
3. A rabbit gets stuck on Wallace's head.
4. Hutch.
5. Brain washes them.
6. Lord Victor Quartermaine.
7. To win Lady Tottington's affection.
8. 24-'carrot' gold bullets.
9. Hutch.
10. Wallace.
11. His precious marrow.
12. A rabbit costume.
13. Philip.
14. Stinking Bishop.
15. A marrow.

Page 72: Wallace and Gromit Quiz

1. Bake-O-Lite bread.
2. Delivering bread.
3. Fluffles.
4. Inventor.
5. He is robotic.
6. Wool shop owner.
7. Campanula.
8. Tottington Hall.
9. PC Mac.
10. Shaun.
11. Crossed cucumbers.
12. A Chicken.
13. NASA.
14. The Cooker.
15. A truncheon.

Page 104: Wallace and Gromit Quiz

1. Green.
2. Red.
3. Cheese.
4. Wensleydale.
5. Wendolene Ramsbottom.
6. Totty.
7. Bread Delivery.
8. Window washing service.
9. Pest control service.
10. Piella Bakewell.
11. Piella was the 'Cereal Killer'.
12. Eaten by crocodiles.
13. With the reward money for capturing Feathers McGraw.
14. Ay-Up!
15. Moon cheese.

Page 106: Wallace and Gromit Quiz

1. Bones.
2. Engineering For Dogs.
3. Dogstoevsky.
4. Bach.
5. Releases the handbrake.
6. A giant diamond.
7. A train set chase!
8. Shaun.
9. Preston.
10. Fluffles.
11. Puppy Love.
12. Hutch.
13. Philip.
14. Shopper 13.
15. A banana.

Waiting for the dough to rise.

Top Bun loafs ready for delivery.

Piella my angel cake.

Piella.

Beautiful bread.

Master baker hard at work.